The American Mosaic
Immigration Today

The Path to Citizenship

Sara Howell

PowerKiDS
press.

New York

Published in 2015 by The Rosen Publishing Group, Inc.
29 East 21st Street, New York, NY 10010

First Edition

Editors: Jennifer Way and Norman D. Graubart
Book Design: Andrew Povolny
Photo Research: Katie Stryker

Photo Credits: Cover Visions of America/Universal Images Group/Getty Images; p. 5 Ariel Skelley/Blend Images/Thinkstock; p. 6 Universal Images Group/Getty Images; p. 7 Viktorya170377/Shutterstock.com; p. 8 nicholas belton/E+/Getty Images; p. 9 Rob Marmion/Shutterstock.com; p. 10 John Moore/Getty Images News/Getty Images; p. 11 Dave Nagel/Stone/Getty Images; p. 12 Otna Ydur/Shutterstock.com; p. 13 Dimtriy Shironosov/iStock/Thinkstock; p. 14 Inti St Clair/Blend Images/Getty Images; p. 15 Jeffrey Coolidge/The Image Bank/Getty Images; p. 16 Daniel Grill/Getty Images; p. 17 Thomas Barwick/Iconica/Getty Images; p. 18 Joe Raedle/Getty Images News/Getty Images; p. 19 Lisa Blumenfeld/Getty Images Sport/Getty Images; p. 20 Bloomberg/Getty Images; p. 21 Digital Vision/Getty Images; p. 22 BlurAZ/Shutterstock.com.

Library of Congress Cataloging-in-Publication Data

Howell, Sara.
 The path to citizenship / by Sara Howell. — First edition.
     pages cm. — (The American mosaic : immigration today)
 Includes index.
 ISBN 978-1-4777-6736-8 (library binding) —
 ISBN 978-1-4777-6737-5 (pbk.) — ISBN 978-1-4777-6648-4 (6-pack)
 1. Citizenship—United States—Juvenile literature. 2. Immigrants—United States—Juvenile literature. 3. Naturalization—United States—Juvenile literature. I. Title.
 JK1759.H646 2015
 323.6'230973—dc23
                                      2013046670

Manufactured in the United States of America

CPSIA Compliance Information: Batch #WS14PK1: For Further Information contact Rosen Publishing, New York, New York at 1-800-237-9932

Contents

Understanding Citizenship

Have you ever wondered what makes someone a **citizen**? There are two ways to become a citizen in the United States. A person who is born in the United States is a US citizen. A person who has a parent who is a US citizen is a citizen, too. A person born in another country can become a US citizen by law through a process called **naturalization**.

Citizenship comes with many rights and responsibilities. For example, citizens in the United States may vote in elections. They also have the right to many important freedoms. This book will explain how people become naturalized citizens of the United States.

There are different ways to become a naturalized citizen. For example, kids under 18 years old become US citizens if a parent becomes a naturalized citizen.

A Nation of Immigrants

Before the United States was formed, groups of Native Americans lived throughout North America. We can think of the first European settlers to arrive in the land as the first **immigrants**. An immigrant is a person who moves from one country to another. The United States is often called a nation of immigrants. While some came hundreds of years ago, many others continue to arrive today!

Among the first Europeans to settle in America were the Pilgrims. They came from England on a ship called the *Mayflower*.

The United States

Mexico

Most immigrants who come to America today come from Mexico. More than 140,000 Mexican immigrants became legal permanent residents in America in 2011.

Since the first settlers arrived, many immigrants have come after them. Large waves, or groups, of people have come from countries such as Ireland, China, Italy, and Mexico. Today, many immigrants come from Mexico, China, India, and the Philippines.

Coming to the United States

Each year, millions of people come to the United States. Some are just visiting for a short time. Others are planning to stay and begin the path to citizenship. Before arriving in the United States, foreign visitors and immigrants must get a **visa**. A visa allows a person to enter the country for a certain amount of time.

Many people need travel visas if they want to visit the United States. Citizens of some countries, like Canada, do not need travel visas to visit.

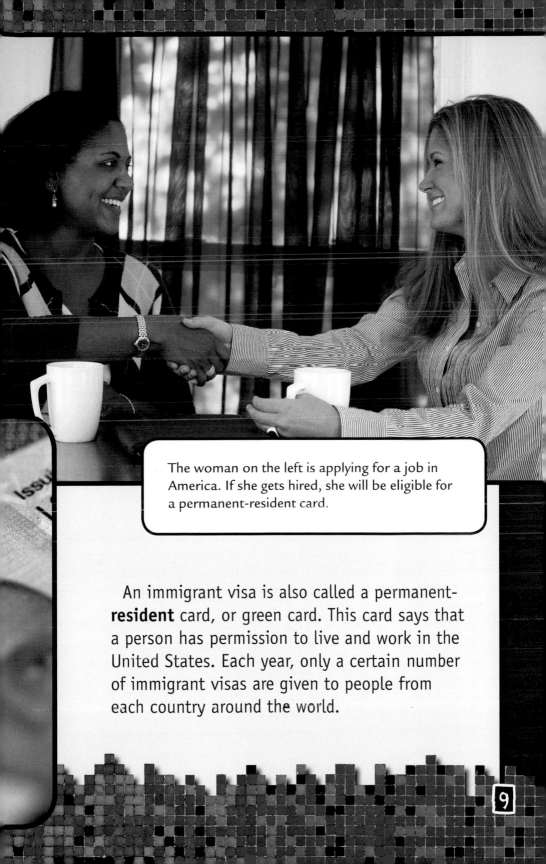

The woman on the left is applying for a job in America. If she gets hired, she will be eligible for a permanent-resident card.

An immigrant visa is also called a permanent-**resident** card, or green card. This card says that a person has permission to live and work in the United States. Each year, only a certain number of immigrant visas are given to people from each country around the world.

Many Paths to Citizenship

The part of the government that handles citizenship is called US Citizenship and Immigration Services. Its website can give you very important information about becoming a US citizen.

To be **eligible** for citizenship, a person must first enter the United States lawfully with an immigrant visa. She must then live in the United States as a permanent resident for at least five years. A person may also be eligible if he lives in the United States for three years and is married to a US citizen.

Another way to become eligible for citizenship is to serve in the US military. A person may also be eligible for citizenship if one of his parents became a naturalized US citizen before he turned 18 years old.

Immigrants can become citizens if they join the military. The military includes the Army, the Navy, the Marines, the Air Force, and the Coast Guard.

Applying for Citizenship

To apply for citizenship, a person fills out a form called the Application for Naturalization. This form asks for information such as where a person went to school and what jobs she has held. The applicant will also need a passport-style photo taken of her face. She will send two copies of the photo, the Application for Naturalization, and a fee, or payment, to US Citizenship and Immigration Services (USCIS).

In 2011, 694,193 people were naturalized. That's a lot of paperwork for USCIS! Sometimes, it can take a long time for citizenship applications to be processed.

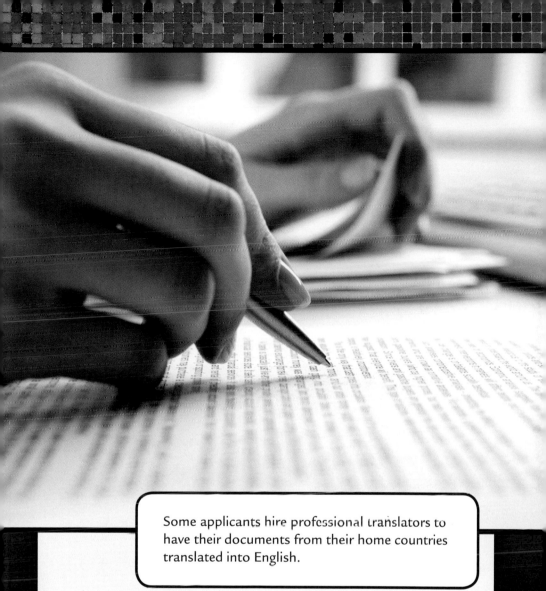

Some applicants hire professional translators to have their documents from their home countries translated into English.

Any other important **documents**, such as marriage licenses, should be sent to USCIS, too. If any documents are in a language other than English, they need to be translated before they are sent.

Character Check

One important **qualification** for citizenship is good moral **character**. This means that a person is honest and has not been in trouble with the law. To find out more about an applicant's history, the government does a background check.

Being honest in your paperwork is important. It is against the law to make false statements on a government document.

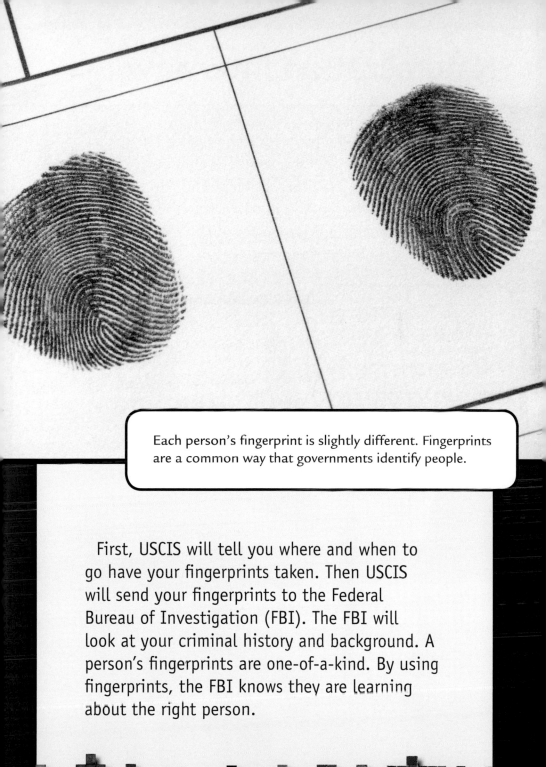

Each person's fingerprint is slightly different. Fingerprints are a common way that governments identify people.

First, USCIS will tell you where and when to go have your fingerprints taken. Then USCIS will send your fingerprints to the Federal Bureau of Investigation (FBI). The FBI will look at your criminal history and background. A person's fingerprints are one-of-a-kind. By using fingerprints, the FBI knows they are learning about the right person.

Naturalization Interview

Once your application has been read and your background has been checked, it is time for your **interview**. USCIS will let you know the date, time, and place for the interview. When you arrive, a USCIS officer will put you under **oath**. This oath is a promise you make to tell the truth.

This man is taking an oath to tell the truth during the interview. Breaking the oath is a serious crime.

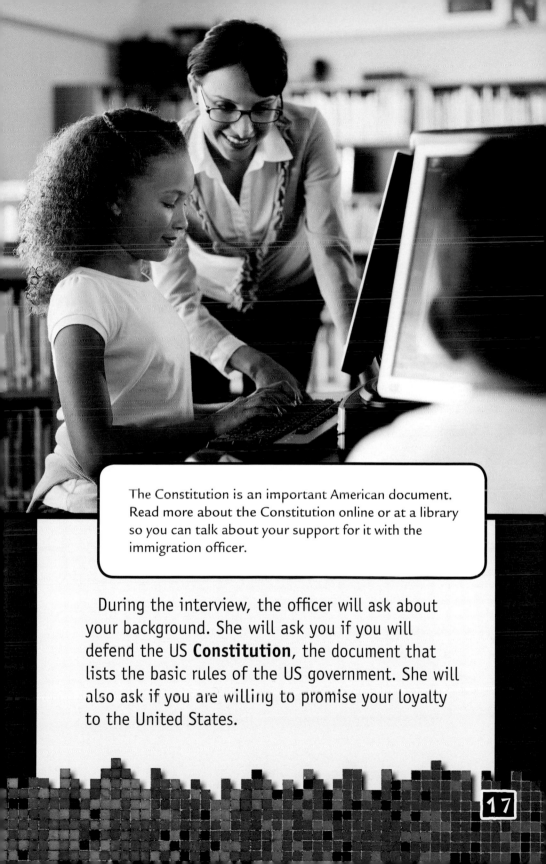

The Constitution is an important American document. Read more about the Constitution online or at a library so you can talk about your support for it with the immigration officer.

During the interview, the officer will ask about your background. She will ask you if you will defend the US **Constitution**, the document that lists the basic rules of the US government. She will also ask if you are willing to promise your loyalty to the United States.

Taking the Test

You can learn English with help from friends and by studying language books. You can also take a class to prepare for the civics test.

During your interview, the USCIS officer will test if you are able to read, speak, and write in English. This is an important qualification for new citizens. She will ask you to read a sentence aloud and write a sentence down.

The officer will also give you a civics test. This test checks to see if you understand how the US government works. It will also test whether you understand your new rights and responsibilities as a US citizen. The officer will ask you 10 questions about the United States. You must get at least six answers correct to pass the test.

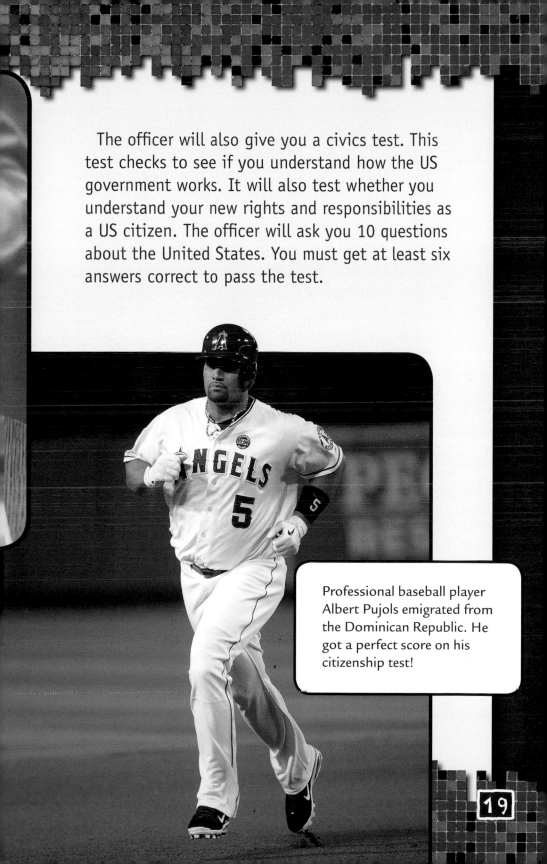

Professional baseball player Albert Pujols emigrated from the Dominican Republic. He got a perfect score on his citizenship test!

A Worthwhile Journey

After the interview, a person's application for citizenship may be approved the very same day! The final step on the path to citizenship is a naturalization **ceremony**, or service. During the ceremony, new citizens make a promise to be loyal to the United States. They are given copies of the Constitution and small American flags.

Naturalization ceremonies can have more than 1,000 new citizens taking the oath at the same time.

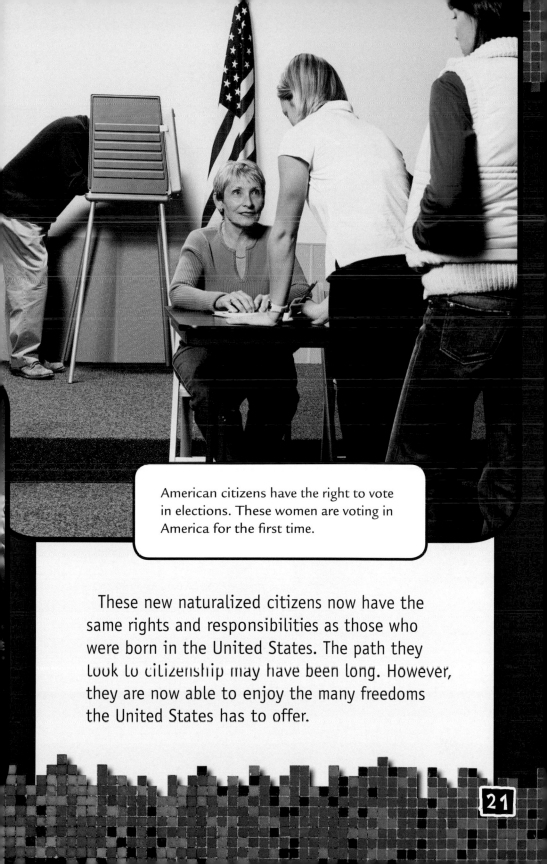

American citizens have the right to vote in elections. These women are voting in America for the first time.

These new naturalized citizens now have the same rights and responsibilities as those who were born in the United States. The path they took to citizenship may have been long. However, they are now able to enjoy the many freedoms the United States has to offer.

The American Mosaic

In the United States, people come from many backgrounds. A picture made by fitting small pieces together to create a larger work of art is called a **mosaic**. In many ways, the United States is a mosaic made up of different people and cultures.

Citizenship is a bond that ties people from different backgrounds and cultures together. Even though they have different beliefs and values, citizens are loyal to their country and work together to make it a better place for everyone!

If you look closely, you will notice that this American flag is made up of many small individual tiles. This is an example of a mosaic.

Glossary

ceremony (SER-ih-moh-nee) A special series of actions done on certain occasions.

character (KER-ik-tur) How a person acts.

citizen (SIH-tih-zen) A person who was born in or has a right to live in a country.

Constitution (kon-stih-TOO-shun) The basic rules by which the United States is governed.

documents (DOK-yoo-ments) Written or printed statements that give official information about something.

eligible (EH-luh-juh-bul) Allowed to participate.

immigrants (IH-muh-grunts) People who move to a new country from another country.

interview (IN-ter-vyoo) When someone questions someone else.

mosaic (moh-ZAY-ik) A picture made by fitting together small pieces of stone, glass, or tile and pasting them in place.

naturalization (na-chuh-ruh-luh-ZAY-shun) The process of becoming a citizen.

oath (OHTH) A promise.

qualification (kwah-luh-fuh-KAY-shun) Requirement.

resident (REH-zih-dent) Someone who lives in a certain place.

visa (VEE-zuh) Official permission to enter a country.

Index

Websites

Due to the changing nature of Internet links, PowerKids Press has developed an online list of websites related to the subject of this book. This site is updated regularly. Please use this link to access the list:

www.powerkidslinks.com/mosa/citiz/